Medusa

Other titles in the Monsters and Mythical Creatures series include:

Aliens
Cyclops
Demons
Dragons
Frankenstein
Goblins
The Mummy
Trolls
Water Monsters
Zombies

Monsters
and Mythical Creatures

Medusa

Kris Hirschmann

ReferencePoint
Press®

San Diego, CA

© 2012 ReferencePoint Press, Inc.
Printed in the United States

For more information, contact:
ReferencePoint Press, Inc.
PO Box 27779
San Diego, CA 92198
www.ReferencePointPress.com

LIBRARY OF CONGRESS CATALOGING-IN-PUBLICATION DATA

Hirschmann, Kris, 1967–
  Medusa / by Kris Hirschmann.
    p. cm. — (Monsters and mythical creatures)
  Includes bibliographical references and index.
  ISBN-13: 978-1-60152-181-1 (hardback : alk. paper)
  ISBN-10: 1-60152-181-2 (hardback : alk. paper) 1. Medusa (Greek mythology) I. Title.
  BL820.M38H57 2012
  398.20938—dc23
                                                                    2011020993

Contents

Introduction

The Face of Mythology

The strapping young hero reaches into a leather bag that hangs at his side. He closes his eyes and then, with one swift motion, pulls the bag's gruesome contents into full view of the assembled crowd. It is a monstrous female head with dead yet somehow angry eyes. The face is twisted into an expression that combines fear, sadness, and profound fury. The hair is a mass of living snakes that writhe and hiss, threatening to bite anyone who approaches.

Yet no one does approach. They cannot because they are rooted to the ground. Everyone present has turned to stone—everyone, that is, except for the youth holding the beastly object. He alone shut his eyes against the creature's gaze, and his life has been spared as a result.

Nearly everyone can name the beast described in this story. The serpent-haired horror is Medusa, a character who figured prominently in the mythology of ancient Greece. Also known as the Gorgon, this fiend has been scaring people for nearly 3,000 years—and she shows no sign of stopping. Today, as in eons past, Medusa holds a place as one of the best-known icons in all of mythology.

There is at least one practical reason for Medusa's recent popularity. Two important mythology collections, Thomas Bulfinch's *Mythology* (1855)

> ## Did You Know?
>
> The head of Medusa appears in the Perseus constellation. The star Altol represents Medusa's eye.

and Edith Hamilton's *Mythology: Timeless Tales of Gods and Heroes* (1942) have become standard textbooks in many middle-school and high-school curricula. Both of these books include detailed versions of Medusa's story. The original version of Hamilton's book even used the Gorgon as its cover image. Glaring balefully outward, Medusa thus became the face of Greek mythology for generations of students.

Yet there are deeper reasons for the Gorgon's prominence. Medusa is not merely frightening; she is also a rich character with a tragic history. Even better, her tale includes all the elements of

The severed head of Medusa, with its mass of writhing snakes and its bulging, angry eyes, presents a haunting image of the mythological being that turns people to stone. Shown here is an early seventeenth-century painting by the Flemish artist Peter Paul Rubens.

great fiction. Birth, death, betrayal, revenge, love, and loss are all wrapped into Medusa's life story. The result is that people simply cannot forget this captivating legend—or its vile villainess. Monstrous and monstrously memorable, the Gorgon Medusa will surely slither her way through the world of mythology for many centuries yet to come.

Chapter 1

Making a Monster

Many thousands of years ago musical storytellers, called bards, were plying their trade throughout ancient Greece. Bards found employment at festivals, in wealthy private homes, and even in town squares. They captivated audiences by recounting traditional Greek stories, events, and legends, all from memory. Part entertainers and part historians, the bards were a key source of information about Greece's past.

Around 800 BC, though, this situation started to change. The art of writing, which had been lost for a time due to a destructive war, began to reemerge. Soon afterward scholars started to create a written record of Greece's rich legacy. The bards' songs and tales were part of this legacy. For the first time ever, Greek gods, heroes, and monsters found their way onto the printed page.

One of these monsters was a fearsome creature called the Gorgon. In the earliest Greek writings, this beast was mentioned only in passing. As the centuries went by, however, the Gorgon became more and more prominent. It developed new physical traits and abilities. It got a family history and became known as a female. The monster also earned a name: Medusa.

Today just about everyone knows this name, and most people can picture the creature to which it belonged. Yet to fully understand Medusa, it is necessary to revisit the monster's origins in Greek literature and legend. Piece by piece, these sources build a complete picture of an ancient menace.

The Works of Homer

The Gorgon first appeared in the works of the blind Greek poet known as Homer. The creature made her literary debut in an epic poem called the *Iliad*, which was probably written sometime between 800 and 750 BC. The events of this poem occur during a great, mythical conflict called the Trojan War. The Gorgon shows up two times in the *Iliad* as a symbol of military strength and fear.

The first mention occurs when the goddess Athena is arming herself for battle. She dons a supernatural garment, called an aegis, that is meant to terrify her opponents. Here is Homer's description of this frightful item: "[It was] wreathed round with Rout [Defeat] as with a fringe, and on it were Strife, and Strength, and Panic whose blood runs cold; moreover there was the head of the dread monster Gorgon, grim and awful to behold."[1]

Did You Know?

Scholars suspect that the Greek tale of Medusa might have sprung from the gods of other ancient cultures. Key "suspects" include the Egyptian god Bes and certain Asian deities.

Later in the poem, a commander named Agamemnon uses the Gorgon's image in a similar way. Preparing to invade Troy, Agamemnon picks up his shield. On this shield, writes Homer, "there were twenty bosses of white tin, with another of dark [blue] in the middle: this last was made to show a Gorgon's head, fierce and grim, with Rout and Panic on either side."[2]

These passages only concern the Gorgon's image. In the *Odyssey*, another epic poem that Homer wrote several decades after the *Iliad*, the beast herself appears—or threatens to, at least. At one point in this poem, a war hero named Odysseus must enter the underworld to talk to the dead. He speaks to many phantoms but is finally scared away by the mere thought of the Gorgon:

"So many thousands of ghosts came round me and uttered such appalling cries, that I was panic stricken lest [the queen of the underworld] should send up from the house of Hades the head of that

awful monster Gorgon. On this I hastened back to my ship and ordered my men to go on board."[3]

It is worth noting that Homer does not actually describe the Gorgon in any of these passages. He seems to assume that his readers already know about the monster. It is clear from this fact that Homer did not invent the Gorgon. He was reusing a character that was already well established in traditional tales.

Expanding the Story

Luckily for modern scholars, these tales were written down in greater detail as time went on. Little by little, Medusa came to life on the printed page.

The Gorgon Medusa first appeared in the works of Homer (pictured) sometime between 800 and 750 BC. In Homer's epic poem The Iliad, *Medusa symbolizes military strength and fear.*

The Origins of a Nightmare

Gorgon-like images appear in the artwork of countless unrelated ancient cultures. Many scholars have tried to understand this puzzling coincidence. They have proposed a variety of explanations for Medusa's worldwide presence.

Author Stephen R. Wilk offers an especially convincing argument. Wilk feels that the ancient Gorgons of all cultures must have been inspired by a universal human experience. He believes that the processes of death and decomposition, which occur in exactly the same way everywhere, are the source of this inspiration.

In his book *Medusa: Solving the Mystery of the Gorgon*, Wilk explains his theory:

> The [Gorgon] is terrible because it shows us the transformation of a human being into Death. . . . The eyes pop out and may cross, the tongue protrudes, the skin discolors and spots, the body bloats, the hair separates, and the entire thing stinks.
>
> In the stylized image of this process . . . the more repugnant aspects have been cleaned up. The eyes are piercing, but not disgusting. They do not cross in a ridiculous way. The protruding tongue is neater. The bloating has been rendered in neat form as a broad nose and wide cheeks. The separating hair has become neat curls, the skin blemishes regular marks and lines. It has been made acceptable.
>
> Acceptable, perhaps—but still frightening. Glaring stonily at the world, Medusa's frozen images keep their owner's memory alive.

Stephen R. Wilk, *Medusa: Solving the Mystery of the Gorgon*. New York: Oxford University Press, 2000, p. 190.

A work called *The Shield of Heracles* is one good example of this trend. Written by a Greek poet named Hesiod around 700 BC, this epic poem touches on Medusa's death at the hands of a human hero. It also mentions that Medusa had two sisters, and it describes aspects of the sisters' horrible appearance. "Two serpents hung down at their girdles with heads curved forward: their tongues were flickering, and their teeth gnashing with fury, and their eyes glaring fiercely,"[4] Hesiod writes.

Another one of Hesiod's works, *Theogony*, provides further details about Medusa and her beastly siblings. It specifies the monsters' names, their dwelling place, and parts of their history. It also lays out the Gorgons' relationship with certain gods. Facts like these were probably well known during Hesiod's lifetime. In later centuries, however, they would certainly have been forgotten if not for written records. Hesiod's poems therefore filled many holes in the Medusa myth.

> # Did You Know?
> No one is certain that the poet known as Homer was an actual man. Some scholars believe that Homer's works were actually created by many poets, over many years.

Filling the Holes

Sometime near the beginning of the Christian era (AD 0–present), an Italian writer named Ovid decided to fill *all* of the holes. Drawing from the works of Hesiod and others, Ovid penned a fairly complete version of Medusa's story. He included the tale in a collection called *Metamorphoses*, which was an encyclopedia of more than 200 ancient legends. This work is an important guide to many Greek gods and monsters, including the Gorgon.

The best guide of all, though, was yet to come. According to scholars, the longest and most accurate Medusa legend ever written appeared around the second century AD in a work called simply the *Library*. Attributed to a Greek scholar named Apollodorus, the *Library*'s version of the Medusa tale includes more details than any other retelling. Apollodorus did not make up these details. He compiled them from several older works and then assembled them into an accurate and very comprehensive version of the Medusa myth.

This approach has been hugely helpful to modern scholars. As one historian notes, "The virtue of [Apollodorus's] work is that he recorded faithfully the details of mythology from whatever sources he found, without seeking to rewrite them himself. . . . His book is thus an incredible treasure, because it has 'frozen' many important myths in older form and conveyed them without change to us."[5] Thanks to its painstaking accuracy, Apollodorus's *Library* stands today as the best single source of Medusa information.

Did You Know?

The offspring of Phorkys and Keto, including Medusa, are known collectively as the Phorcydes, in reference to their father's name.

Yet the *Library* is by no means the only source. Many ancient writers mentioned Medusa in passing. They provided facts that helped to describe the Gorgon. By assembling tidbits from multiple sources, modern historians have formed a detailed profile of Greece's most terrifying monster.

Medusa's Family Tree

This profile begins with Medusa's family tree. The Gorgon's story starts literally at the dawn of creation, when the earth goddess Gaia emerged from Chaos. Alone and lonely, Gaia created several other gods to keep her company. She took the sea god, Pontus, as her companion.

Many children arose from the union of Gaia and Pontus. Two of these children were named Phorkys and Keto—and these two were a terrifying pair indeed. Phorkys was a red-skinned merman with a scaly tail and lobster-like feet and horns. His sister Keto appeared more human, but she kept fearsome company. As the goddess of whales, large sharks, and sea monsters, Keto personified the ocean's most dangerous residents.

Although they were siblings, Phorkys and Keto wed. Together they produced many offspring who, not surprisingly, were nearly as monstrous as their parents. One child, Echidna, was half nymph and half viper. She became known as "the Mother of All Monsters" because she gave birth to so many other horrible creatures. Another child, Ladon, was a snake-like dragon who guarded a mythological orchard.

A set of triplets called the Graeae were also the children of Phorkys and Keto. Sometimes called the gray sisters or the gray witches, these goddesses were broken-down old women even at birth. They lived together beyond the boundaries of the human world. Forced to share a single tooth and eye, the sisters bickered constantly about whose turn it was to see and eat.

The Graeae were not the only triplets in the family. A much more frightening trio of sisters lived nearby. Named Euryale (which means "Far Roaming"), Sthenno (which means "Forceful"), and Medusa (which means "Guardian"), this group was infinitely more intimidating than the elderly, hapless Graeae. Known collectively as the Gorgons, these sisters were truly monstrous in appearance. They were also angry and vicious, and they had terrifying supernatural abilities. With these traits, the Gorgons added a touch of true horror to the family tree.

From Human to Horrible

Two of the Gorgons, Euryale and Sthenno, were awful creatures from the moment of their birth. Medusa, however, was a bit different. She looked like a human woman when she was born—and a stunningly gorgeous one at that. Ovid mentions this fact in his *Metamorphoses*. "Beyond all others she was famed for beauty. . . . Words would fail to tell the glory of her hair, most wonderful of all her charms,"[6] he writes.

This beauty did not go unnoticed. Medusa soon caught the eye of Poseidon, the god of the sea. Smitten, Poseidon pursued the lovely Gorgon relentlessly. Some sources say that Poseidon eventually won Medusa's favor. Others say that the sea god forced his attentions onto his intended conquest. Either way, the moment of seduction occurred inside a temple devoted to the goddess Athena. Some writers claim that it took place on the goddess's very altar.

Unfortunately, this was the worst possible place for a romantic tryst. Athena was a virgin goddess, known for her purity and modesty. She was deeply offended by the misuse of her temple. She could not permit this disrespectful act to go unchallenged. Yet Athena had a problem. Poseidon was powerful—too powerful, in fact, to be much affected by anything Athena could do. He was also male and a god. In the Greek tradition, male deities got away with every imaginable type of bad behavior. They were seldom blamed for their actions.

For all of these reasons, Athena's wrath was directed at Medusa alone. The goddess used her powers to change Medusa into a monster, much like her sisters. She paid special attention to the Gorgon's glorious tresses. As Ovid says, "[Athena] changed the Gorgon's splendid hair to serpents horrible."[7] Medusa's locks would never again tempt any man—god or mortal—toward indelicate thoughts or deeds.

A Frightful Trio

It is no surprise that Medusa now unnerved her former suitors. The newly snake-haired monster was fearsome to behold. One writer describes her visage with these words: "The Gorgon's head . . . was a frightening object, with eyes starting out of their sockets, and serpentine hair about the temples all writhing and erect."[8]

The snakes were dreadful indeed. Yet they were not the Gorgon's only terrifying trait. Like her sisters, Medusa had a monstrous body to go along with her horrible hair. Apollodorus described the awful triplets in one chilling passage: "The Gorgons had heads twined about with the scales of dragons, and great tusks like swine's, and brazen hands, and golden wings, by which they flew."[9]

Medusa's hideous Gorgon sisters pursue Perseus, the son of the Greek god Zeus and a mortal woman, in this Charles Kingsley illustration from 1928. The Gorgons—Euryale, Sthenno, and Medusa—possessed terrifying supernatural abilities.

From this description, it seems clear that the Gorgons were dangerous creatures indeed. They had all the tools they needed to pursue humans and rip them to shreds. Luckily for the human population, though, the Gorgons were not hunters. They kept to themselves, making their home in a miserable cave far from any human or godly circles. This cave, explains Hesiod, lay "beyond the famous stream of the Ocean . . . in the utmost place toward night."[10]

At first only Euryale and Sthenno lived in this remote location. The lovely Medusa was welcome in more civilized circles. After her monstrous transformation, however, Medusa joined her sisters at the edge of the world. This isolation was an important safety measure because Medusa, unlike her sister Gorgons, was mortal. She was in constant danger of being hunted and killed by adventurous human heroes.

Turned to Stone

The heroes did come. Yet Medusa and her sisters were far from helpless against these intruders. All of the Gorgons possessed terrifying strength, speed, and cunning. Even worse, they had the power to turn living creatures to stone. A single glance at Medusa's snake-ringed face meant a rocky death for any person or animal that approached.

During the first century AD, a Spanish writer named Lucan graphically described this fate in a work called the *Pharsalia*:

> Nobody ever felt fear as he gazed at that monster's grinning face, because he had no time to feel any emotion whatsoever. One could not even describe what happened to him as death, for being prevented from gasping out his spirit, this became petrified with his body. . . . [Medusa] had the extraordinary power of paralyzing everything in sea, in sky, or on earth by turning it to stone. Birds suddenly grew heavy and crashed to the ground; beasts stood frozen on their rocks; entire tribes of [people] were transformed to statues. No living creature, in fact, could bear to look at that face, not even the serpents on her head.[11]

Considering this effect, it makes sense that Medusa's home range was a desolate place, rocky and barren. Most living creatures avoided it at all costs—and those who did not paid a high price for their foolishness. The approach to the Gorgons' lair was littered with the statue-like remains of lions, human soldiers, and other creatures who had ventured just a bit too close.

Yet animals and people were not the only beings affected in this way. The gods also were vulnerable to Medusa's petrifying power. Ovid addresses this fact in a tale of mighty Atlas, a god doomed to hold the sky on his shoulders forever. As the story goes, Atlas tried one day to drive a human away from his garden. He did not know that the man possessed Medusa's severed head. The angry man whipped the Gorgon's head out of a bag and held it up toward Atlas. Immediately, says Ovid, "Atlas, huge and vast, becomes a mountain—His great beard and hair are forests, and his shoulders and his hands mountainous ridges, and his head the top of a high peak;—his bones are changed to rocks."[12]

> ## Did You Know?
> Medusa and other Greek gods and goddesses who had links to the underworld were known as chthonic deities, from the Greek word *chthonios*, which means "in or under the earth."

The result of this transformation can still be seen today. The Atlas Mountains, a range that stretches more than 1,500 miles (2,500km) across parts of northern Africa, are said to be the petrified remains of the god Atlas. Thousands of years after Medusa's story was first told, these mighty peaks still hold up the sky—just as they will do for thousands of years yet to come.

Bloody Powers

According to folklore, the Atlas Mountains region is not merely rocky because of Medusa's influence. It is also infested with venomous snakes. The nearby Libyan deserts, where cobras and other deadly reptiles abound, are particularly affected by the Gorgon's powers.

The Downlooker

Several ancient sources say that the Gorgon was not merely a mythical creature. They claim that the legend of Medusa sprang from a true—and truly horrifying—animal. A writer named Atheneaus described this awful beast sometime around AD 200.

The gorgon is the creature which the Numidians of Libya, where it occurs, call the "downlooker.". . . It is like a wild sheep; but some say that it is like a calf. They say, too, that it has a breath so strong that it destroys anyone who meets the animal. And it carries a mane hanging from its forehead over the eyes; whenever it shakes this aside, as it does with difficulty because of its weight, and catches sight of anything, it kills whatever is seen by it; not by its breath, but by the influence which emanates from the peculiar nature of its eyes; and it turns the object into a corpse. . . .

Some soldiers . . . saw the gorgon, and supposing it was a wild sheep, since its head was bent low and it moved slowly, they rushed forward to get it, thinking they could kill it with what swords they had. But the creature, being startled, shook the mane which lay over its eyes and immediately turned to corpses the men who had rushed upon it. Again and again other persons did the same thing and became corpses.

Atheneaus, *The Deipnosophistae*, vol. 2, bk. 5. Cambridge, MA: Harvard University Press, 1928, pp. 502–03.

The snake situation did not arise from Medusa's glance. It was caused by the monster's blood, which was cursed along with the rest of its owner. Legend has it that the blood dripped onto the desert sands when the Gorgon's severed head was carried above. As Ovid writes, "Drops from the Gorgon's head fell bloody on the ground, and earth received them, turning them into vipers. For this reason Libya, today, is full of deadly serpents."[13]

Medusa's blood had other terrible effects as well. For instance, some writers suggest that this fluid, like the Gorgon's face, could turn things to stone. In one ancient story Medusa's severed head bleeds onto a pile of seaweed on the shore of the Red Sea. The sea-weed instantly becomes coral. In a slightly different version of the tale, Medusa's head falls into the ocean and tumbles about on the sea floor, leaving a bloody trail as it rolls. This trail hardens into coral reefs that still exist today.

A few times in Greek my-thology, Medusa's blood comes into direct contact with humans. The results are generally unpleas-ant because blood drawn from the Gorgon's left side was imme-diately and fatally poisonous to mortals. The goddess Athena took advantage of this fact by collect-ing Medusa's blood after the Gordon died. She used drops of this deathly liquid to dispatch various enemies.

> # Did You Know?
>
> The word *gorgon* comes from the Greek word *gorgós*, which means "dreadful."

Interestingly, blood drawn from the Gorgon's right side had ex-actly the opposite effect. This fluid was a powerful healing potion that could cure any human ailment. It could even bring the dead back to life. It is said that Asclepius, a Greek healer who later be-came a god, used the Gorgon's blood for this purpose.

The Power to Terrify

The reference to Asclepius raises an interesting point about the Medusa mystique. The Gorgon was unquestionably deadly. Han-dled properly, however, she could actually help people instead of hurting them. Her monstrous powers could be channeled in positive ways.

This idea eventually made its way into the superstitions of ancient Greece. Over the centuries people came to believe that Medusa's image had protective abilities. In particular, they thought her face could ward off evil powers and other supernatural threats.

Modern scholars are intrigued by the Gorgon's gradual change from monster to protector. "The head of Medusa [is] transformed into a beneficial emblem and a source of civic and martial strength. . . . [It wards off] the evils it embodies. Terror is used to drive out terror, so that the formerly stupefying image is turned back upon one's enemies,"[14] note the editors of a collection of many Medusa-related works.

It is an interesting reversal but also a logical one. The Gorgon is a terrifying creature with terrifying powers. By displaying images of Medusa's head, people hoped to harness these powers in some small way. The gruesome Gorgon, after all, frightened even the gods. Perhaps she could also scare away natural disasters, otherworldly evils, or even plain old bad luck.

This superstitious behavior probably had little or no effect, but it made people feel better and gave them a sense of control over the unknown. And Medusa, had she been real, surely would have been happy to help. Spurned and punished by the gods, the Gorgon would have seized any opportunity to take revenge against her enemies. Medusa's survival on everyday objects means that now, more than 3,000 years after her mythological birth, the monster is still alive in humankind's imagination. And no revenge could be sweeter than that.

Chapter 2

Perseus and Medusa

Medusa makes many passing appearances in ancient Greek literature. The Gorgon's biggest moment, however, occurs during the story of a hero named Perseus. Told at length by Apollodorus and Ovid and mentioned by many other writers, this tale explains why and how Perseus sought the Gorgon. It also describes the many dreadful results of Perseus's successful quest.

The story of Perseus and Medusa stands out in Greek mythology. It is a true classic of the genre, bulging with gods, monsters, magic, and mayhem. Ancient though it is, today this story is just as exciting—and just as horrifying—as it was in long-ago times.

The Story Begins

Medusa's tale begins far from the Gorgon's lair in a Greek city called Argos. This city was ruled by a king named Acrisius. Acrisius's daughter, Danaë, consorted with the god Zeus. As the result of this union, Danaë bore a son named Perseus.

This event horrified Acrisius. An oracle had told the king that he would be killed one day by a grandson. Perseus's birth was therefore a very unwelcome development. To keep himself safe, the king shut Danaë and Perseus into a chest and cast it into the sea. He prayed that the ocean tides would wash the chest far, far away from Argos—far enough, in fact, that Acrisius would never see Danaë or Perseus again.

The tides did their job. They carried the chest out of the Bay of Argos and into the Mediterranean Sea. After days of drifting, the chest approached the tiny island of Seriphos. It was pulled out of the sea and opened by a fisherman named Diktys, who took pity on poor Danaë and her infant son. Diktys gave the pair a home and raised Perseus as his own son. Happy and safe in the fisherman's house, Perseus grew uneventfully to manhood.

Perseus's quiet life, however, was about to change forever. Diktys had a brother, Polydektes, who was the king of Seriphos. Polydektes saw the lovely Danaë one day—and he wanted her. He vowed to make Danaë his wife.

Seeking Medusa's Head

Polydektes, however, ran into trouble with this plan. Danaë did not want to marry the king. Supporting his mother's wishes, the now-adult Perseus turned Polydektes away. His exact actions are never explained. Apollodorus makes it clear, though, that Perseus is the main roadblock to Polydektes's wishes. "[Polydektes] could not get access to her, because Perseus was grown to man's estate,"[15] the writer explains.

Perseus's refusal only made Polydektes more determined. The king *would* marry Danaë. If he had to get rid of Perseus first, so be it. To accomplish this goal, Polydektes devised a plan. He called together all of his friends, including Perseus, and told them that he was collecting wedding gifts for one of the island's prominent families. He asked each man to contribute a horse—an expensive item that he suspected Perseus could not afford.

> ## Did You Know?
> Long after his quest for Medusa's head ended, Perseus had a daughter named Gorgophone. This name means "Gorgon Slayer."

Although Polydektes had only meant to shame Perseus with this request, he got much more than he had bargained for. Young, brash, and eager to impress, Perseus boasted that he could do better than a mere horse. He declared that he would fulfill *any* request and "would not stick even at the Gorgon's head."[16]

The king was dumbstruck by his luck. His hated opponent had just volunteered to enter a monster's lair! The words had been uttered in jest, but Polydektes did not care. He immediately accepted Perseus's foolish offer.

Too late, Perseus realized his mistake. He tried to bring Polydektes a horse, as the other men were doing, but Polydektes refused this gift. He insisted that Perseus obtain Medusa's head instead, as promised—and Perseus had to comply. As one scholar explains, "There never seems to have been any question that Perseus could substitute something else for the head, or not appear at the gathering at all. This, apparently, was a matter of honor, and Perseus would have to succeed in bringing back the head of the Gorgon or die in the attempt."[17]

Divine Gifts

Death, unfortunately, was the most likely outcome of this adventure. Perseus knew that many heroes had tried to kill Medusa. He did not know exactly what had happened to these heroes. No one did—because not a single one of them had returned.

Sickened by his plight, Perseus wandered into the wilderness. He was sitting alone, wondering what to do, when the messenger god, Hermes, happened to pass overhead. Hermes spotted Perseus and noticed how sad he looked. Knowing that the young man was Zeus's son, Hermes descended to find out what was wrong.

Gods often spoke with mortals in those days, so Perseus was only moderately surprised when Hermes appeared before him. The youth explained his plight to the wing-footed deity. After hearing Perseus's story, Hermes told the young man not to worry. He thought he could help—and he knew a goddess who might want to help as well.

Hermes then summoned Athena. The goddess was still angry at Medusa for her indiscretion with Poseidon, and she leaped at the opportunity to do further harm to the Gorgon. She eagerly agreed to help Perseus accomplish his bloody goal.

Medusa's Offspring

The original myth of Perseus and Medusa includes a little-known fact: The Gorgon was pregnant with Poseidon's twins when Perseus struck his fatal blow. These twins were born from Medusa's neck at the moment she was beheaded. This fact is first revealed in Hesiod's *Theogony*. "And when Perseus cut off [Medusa's] head, there sprang forth great Chrysaor and the horse Pegasus who is so called because he was born near the springs (pegae) of Ocean; and that other, because he held a golden blade (aor) in his hands," the poet writes.

Despite his remarkable birth, Chrysaor does not play a large role in Greek mythology. He may have been a king of Iberia at one point. He seems to have fathered a son named Geryon. Other than these details, little is known about this character.

Chrysaor's twin brother, on the other hand, rose to considerable prominence in the Greek pantheon. The winged horse Pegasus became a favorite among the gods and participated in many heroic adventures. He eventually earned immortality when the god Zeus changed him into a constellation and placed him in the sky. Thanks to this story and others, Medusa's son Pegasus has earned a spot—just like his mother before him—as one of the best-known creatures in all of mythology.

Hesiod, *Theogony*, in *The Homeric Hymns and Homerica*, trans. Hugh G. Evelyn-White. Cambridge, MA: Harvard University Press, 1982, Theoi Greek Mythology. www.theoi.com.

There was just one small problem. Athena and Hermes could not help Perseus directly. The youth would have to kill the Gorgon on his own. The gods *could*, however, provide guidance. They could also make sure Perseus had the tools he needed to succeed in his quest.

To this end, Hermes gave Perseus a curved blade made of a material called adamant. This substance, which appears in many ancient Greek stories, is not found anywhere in the real world. It is a supernaturally hard material, stronger than diamonds. Gods used it to make chains, weapons, and other things that required extreme durability. Perseus's adamantine sickle, as it is usually called, was intended to be used to behead the Gorgon. The weapon needed to be unusually strong and sharp, so adamant was the perfect choice.

Next Hermes and Athena gave Perseus some advice. They told him to seek the Graeae, who were the Gorgons' sisters. Only the Graeae knew where to find the Hesperides, a group of nymphs who owned several items that Perseus would need in his quest. Perseus would have to convince the Graeae to provide this information.

Perseus and the Graeae

So Perseus set off in search of the Graeae. He soon found the sisters in their lair at the edge of the world. The Graeae, who were named Enyo, Pemphredo, and Dino, were old women who shared a single tooth and a single eye. They took turns using these items. This meant that while one sister could see and chew, the other two were blind and toothless.

Perseus decided to take advantage of this situation. He lurked quietly near the Graeae, listening to their conversation and watching their actions. He took great care not to be spotted by the sister with the eye. Soon the time came for someone else to use the eye and the tooth. One sister plucked these items from her head and held them out to her siblings. For the moment, all three Graeae were sightless— and this is when Perseus made his move. He swooped in and snatched the precious objects from the old woman's outstretched hand. Then he backed away and waited for the Graeae to notice their loss.

They did, quickly, and they all began to howl. They begged Perseus to return their most treasured possessions. Perseus replied that

> # Did You Know?
> Psychoanalyst Sigmund Freud thought that the myth of Perseus and Medusa had a deeper meaning. He thought it represented universal male anxieties about powerful females.

he would gladly return the items—if the Graeae would direct him to the Hesperides.

This request presented a dilemma for the Graeae. The sisters were not supposed to give out the information Perseus sought. Yet the hags could not imagine spending the rest of eternity without

Guided by the hand of the goddess Athena, Perseus cuts off Medusa's head. He avoids turning to stone by looking at Medusa's reflection in his shield rather than looking directly at her, as depicted in this seventeenth-century painting by artist Baldassare Franceschini.

their eye and their tooth. Feeling they had little choice, the Graeae told Perseus where to find the nymphs.

Different sources give different versions of what happened next. Apollodorus says that Perseus returned the Graeae's possessions as promised. "When the [Graeae] had shown him the way, he gave them back the tooth and the eye,"[18] Apollodorus writes. Other writers, however, say that Perseus did *not* return the eye. He tossed it into nearby Lake Tritonis, leaving the Graeae permanently blind. He did this to make sure that the gray-haired sisters could not chase him as he continued his quest.

Visiting the Nymphs

After leaving the home of the Graeae, Perseus traveled even farther from human civilization. He eventually reached the Hesperides's home, which was a lush garden near the Atlas Mountains. Here the carefree nymphs passed long, lazy days, amusing themselves with countless silly diversions.

Perseus's arrival caused quite a stir among the bored nymphs. The Hesperides seldom had guests, and they wanted to play with their handsome visitor. Perseus teasingly promised the nymphs that he would frolic all they wanted—later. Right now, though, he needed their help. The young man explained his quest and asked politely for assistance.

The smitten nymphs were all too happy to comply. They gave Perseus winged sandals, so he could fly to the Gorgon's lair. They also provided a magical bag or wallet called a *kibisis*. According to various sources, the *kibisis* could grow to hold any object of any size. The nymphs told Perseus to place the Gorgon's head, once he obtained it, into this secure container.

The nymphs also gave Perseus a third gift: an object called the cap of Hades. Hades was the ruler of the Greek underworld. His cap

> # Did You Know?
> The myth of Perseus and Medusa takes place in many real-life locations. Perseus's birthplace, the city of Argos, still stands today. The island of Seriphos is also a real place.

had the extremely useful ability to make its wearer invisible. "[Perseus] put the cap on his head. Wearing it, he saw whom he pleased, but was not seen by others,"[19] Apollodorus explains.

Thus armed, Perseus left the garden of the Hesperides. He ran godlike through the sky on his winged shoes, coming closer and closer to Medusa's home. At some point during this flight Perseus received yet another gift. The goddess Athena gave the young hero a highly polished metal shield. She told Perseus to use the shield as a mirror when he approached Medusa. He could look at the Gorgon's monstrous reflection without fear of turning to stone.

Slaying the Gorgon

Perseus flew to the banks of the river Ocean, a mighty waterway that was said to encircle the mortal realm. The youth knew he was getting close to Medusa's lair when he started to see the remains of the Gorgon's victims. "On all sides, through the fields, along the highways, [Perseus] saw the forms of men and beasts, made stone by one look at Medusa's face,"[20] Ovid writes.

Soon enough Perseus reached the Gorgons' cave. He turned his back to the cave to avoid catching any glimpse of Medusa. Then he brought out Athena's mirrored shield. He held the shield up and angled it until he could clearly see the cave's reflection. Slowly and silently, Perseus stepped backward into the dread tunnel.

What he saw astonished him. There were the Gorgons, lying together still and quiet. The sinister sisters were fast asleep. Even Medusa's serpentine locks were dozing! This was a huge stroke of luck, and Perseus did not hesitate to take advantage of it. He crept backward, step by step, until he was within striking range. He took out the adamantine sickle that Hermes had given him. Then, says Apollodorus, "Perseus stood over them as they slept, and while Athena guided his hand and he looked with averted gaze on a brazen shield, in which he beheld the image of the Gorgon, he beheaded her."[21]

Perseus seized the dripping head and thrust it into the *kibisis*. He ran from the cave with his treasure. Perseus's retreat, unfortu-

Perseus After Medusa

The myth of Perseus does not end with Medusa's death. Apollodorus goes on to explain that the young hero, having dispatched the Gorgon and saved his mother, decides that it is time to meet his grandfather—Danaë's father, King Acrisius. Perseus heads for Argos, intending to introduce himself to the king. Acrisius, however, hears that Perseus is coming and remembers the oracle's dreadful warning. Fearing for his life, the king flees to a neighboring kingdom. There he amuses himself by watching an athletic competition that has drawn youths from all over Greece.

This decision turns out to be Acrisius's undoing. Perseus, finding himself at loose ends when he arrives in Argos and finds the king gone, decides to attend the competition himself. He soon shows up and throws himself joyfully into the games. During one event Perseus is required to toss a discus. The discus flies awry and zooms straight into the crowd, where it strikes and kills Acrisius. In this manner the oracle's prophecy was fulfilled.

nately, was not as quiet as his approach. The sound of the young man's pounding feet woke Medusa's sisters, Euryale and Sthenno, who immediately saw their headless sibling lying dead on the floor. Howling with fury, the sisters leaped up and ran after the fleeing Perseus. "And after him rushed the Gorgons, unapproachable and unspeakable, longing to seize him. . . . And upon the awful heads of the Gorgons great Fear was quaking,"[22] Hesiod writes of this terrible moment.

Once again, though, the gods were on Perseus's side. The youth was wearing the cap of Hades, which made him invisible. He was also wearing the nymphs' winged sandals, which enabled him to fly. With the aid of these shoes, Perseus ran up, up, up into the heavens. The Gorgons also could fly, of course, and they tried their best to follow Medusa's murderer—but thanks to the cap of Hades, they could not see their prey. Unseen and swift, Perseus soon made his escape.

The Rescue of Andromeda

Perseus ran nimbly through the sky, heading for his home island of Seriphos. He was passing over Ethiopia when he spied a maiden chained to a rock. Perseus was curious, so he descended to investigate the situation.

The youth learned that the maiden was a princess named Andromeda. She was chained to the rock because her mother, Cassiopeia, had offended the sea god, Poseidon. To make amends, the queen was offering her daughter as a sacrifice to a sea monster. She hoped that Andromeda's death would appease the angry Poseidon.

Perseus did not like this plan at all. The princess was beautiful—so beautiful, in fact, that Perseus instantly fell in love with her. The young man told Andromeda's father, King Cepheus, that he would rescue the princess if he could marry her afterward. Cepheus could see the monster approaching at that very moment. Feeling he had little choice, the king agreed to Perseus's request. Perseus promptly whipped out a sword and killed the serpent in a short but bloody battle. Triumphant, he turned to Andromeda's parents and demanded his reward.

A Bloody Feast

The wedding feast took place that very night. At first everything went smoothly. As the evening wore on, however, moods turned sour, and harsh words were exchanged. It turned out that before Perseus arrived, Andromeda had been engaged to a man named Phineus. Phineus had not done a thing to help Andromeda earlier that day. Nonetheless, he was furious at Perseus for claiming his bride. After a heated argument, Phineus lost his temper and tried—but failed—to hurl a spear through Perseus's skull.

This act caused a huge battle to break out. Some of the wedding guests fought on Perseus's side. They respected his bravery in killing the sea monster, and they felt he deserved to marry Andromeda. More men, however, remained loyal to Phineus. Outmanned and outarmed, Perseus and his supporters lost ground little by little.

A moment finally came when Perseus knew all was lost. Most of his men had been killed, and Perseus felt his own strength failing. It was time for desperate measures. With his back against a wall and a row of enemies standing before him, Perseus opened the *kibisis* and reached inside. "If any friends are here, then turn away your faces!"[23] he cried. Closing his eyes, Perseus seized the Gorgon's snaky hair and lifted his trophy out of the *kibisis*. He held Medusa's severed head out toward Phineus and his angry mob.

The results were immediate—and horrifying. One by one, Phineus's closest friends turned into stone statues. The effect rippled outward through the wedding crowd, petrifying soldiers on both sides of the battle. The slaughter was mind-numbing. "It would take too long to tell the names of all those who perished; two hundred men survived; at least as many looked at the Gorgon and were turned to stone,"[24] Ovid writes.

Phineus was not among these victims. He was smart enough to see what was happening and avert his eyes. "You win, O Perseus! Take away that monster, that face that makes men stone. . . . I yield,"[25] he groaned.

Perseus, however, was not moved by these words. The youth grimly approached Phineus and once again raised Medusa's head. This time Phineus could not avoid the Gorgon's gaze. "As he struggled to turn his eyes, his neck grew hard, his tears were changed to marble, and in marble still the suppliant look, the pleading hands, the pose, the cringe—all these were caught and fixed forever,"[26] says Ovid. With a single glance from her dead eyes, Medusa permanently ended Phineus's bad behavior.

The Return to Seriphos

After this incident Perseus resumed his homeward journey with his new bride at his side. He was starting to feel a sense of urgency now. He knew he needed to reach Seriphos quickly to help his mother, Danaë, evade the wicked Polydektes.

Perseus's worst fears were realized when he finally reached his home island. Polydektes had assumed that Perseus was dead, and he had tried to force Danaë into marriage. Danaë and Diktys had taken refuge at a local temple to thwart Polydektes's plans. Yet this action did not deter Polydektes in the slightest. The king had assembled a group of friends at the palace, and he was getting ready to pull the pair out of the temple by force.

Perseus had no intention of letting this happen. The fact that he was just one man against many did not bother him. After all, he had been in the same position at his wedding feast. That experience had taught Perseus exactly how to stop an angry mob.

This time there was no great battle. Perseus simply marched into Polydektes' palace and walked straight up to the surprised king. Once again he reached into the *kibisis*. Then, averting his gaze, Perseus pulled out the gruesome contents. The results were predictably monstrous. "He showed the Gorgon's head; and all who beheld it were turned to stone, each in the attitude which he happened to have struck,"[27] writes Apollodorus.

The End of the Tale

At this point Perseus had accomplished all of his goals. He had obtained Medusa's head, and he had saved his mother from an unwanted marriage. Now it was time to move forward.

Perseus's first act was to crown Diktys the king of Seriphos to replace the petrified Polydektes. This was a logical appointment because Polydektes had been Diktys's brother. Diktys apparently ruled

Perseus averts his gaze as he presents the head of Medusa to the wicked king Polydektes in this 1910 illustration. Anyone who actually looked at the gruesome object immediately turned to stone.

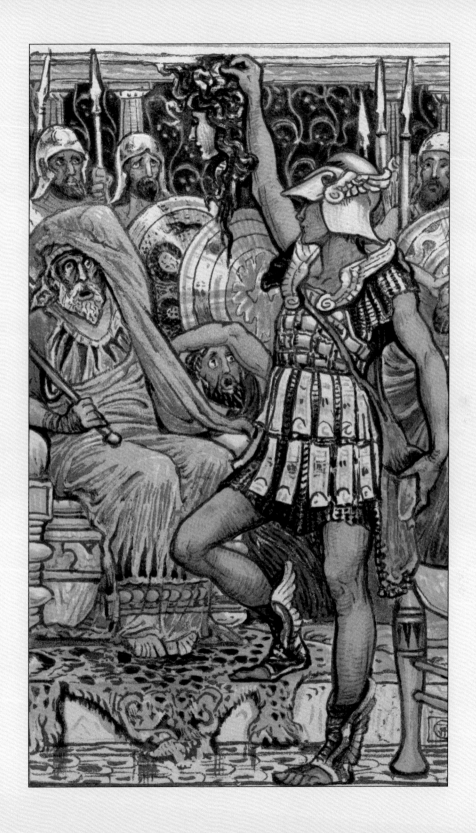

well and wisely because he disappears from the picture at this point. Nothing was ever heard from him again.

Next Perseus had to return the magical objects he had gathered on his quest. He gave the winged sandals, the *kibisis*, and the cap of Hades to the god Hermes. Hermes returned these items to the nymphs, who were their rightful owners.

Medusa's head was the last item to be dealt with. Perseus knew he could not keep such a dangerous object. Yet he was not sure what to do with it, so he asked the goddess Athena for help. This was a good choice because Athena was delighted to take possession of the Gorgon's remains. She mounted the head in the center of her shield, where it could intimidate and even kill her enemies. In this way Medusa's power endured forever on the divine battlefields of Greek mythology.

The Ultimate Revenge

In a storytelling sense, Athena's actions bring Medusa's story to a deliciously satisfying end. The goddess was responsible, after all, for the Gorgon's terrible looks and powers. The fact that Athena ultimately benefited from these awful "gifts" was therefore the greatest possible act of revenge. Athena not only made Medusa monstrous, but she also enslaved her creation by turning her worst traits into personal weapons.

In this battle of wills, then, Athena comes out ahead. Yet in the long term it is Medusa who gets the last laugh. Enduring an eternal life after death on Athena's shield, the Gorgon appeared in every war and at every Olympian gathering. She showed up repeatedly in artwork and in folktales. Over time the Gorgon's staring face became forever linked with the goddess who carried it.

The result is ironic. Athena wanted Medusa dead—but instead, she gave her immortality. Thanks largely to Athena's mythological actions, the story of the Gorgon has already endured for nearly 3,000 years, and it will undoubtedly endure for many more centuries. Creepy yet compelling, this ancient Greek monster will continue to find a place in modern nightmares.

Chapter 3

Medusa in Art, Literature, and Theater

G reek mythology is quite clear about Medusa's fate: The Gorgon dies when Perseus beheads her. Consigned to the underworld, the snake-haired monster never again troubles the mortal population.

So the legendary Medusa was permanently dispatched. The idea of the Gorgon, however, has turned out to be harder to kill. Between her terrifying looks, her awesome powers, and her tragic history, Medusa has captured the public imagination in a way that few other monsters before—or since—have managed.

It seems that creative people of all types are especially fascinated by the Gorgon. Medusa is featured prominently in the art, literature, and theater of many cultures and eras. Appearing in a vast range of works, from paintings to plays and architecture to operas, the Gorgon has found a new life in many different artistic genres.

The Gorgoneia

The oldest of these genres might be termed *everyday art*. As early as 800 BC images of Medusa's staring face started to appear on cups, bowls, vases, doors, coins, tombstones, and other common items throughout ancient Greece. Today these images are known collectively as Gorgoneia. Clearly meant to represent the Medusa of legend, Gorgoneia were a staple of the region's decorating trends.

It is very easy to recognize early, or archaic, Gorgoneia, as scholars call them. These images tend to be remarkably similar. They are free-floating heads without bodies or even necks. The faces are round, with bulging eyes, broad noses, and prominent cheeks. The mouths are wide, and they hang partly open to reveal fang-like upper and lower teeth. A swollen, protruding tongue sticks out between the monster's thick lips. Atop the head is a mass of curly hair that presumably represents the snakes of ancient legend.

Scholar Stephen R. Wilk points out another feature that most ancient Gorgoneia share. "Unlike almost any other mythological

The snake-covered head of Medusa is the subject of this mosaic from ancient Rome. The Gorgon's image appears on cups, vases, coins, and other items from the ancient world.

creature, it is always presented full-face, glaring directly [outward]," he explains. "Even in later Greek and Roman art, it was rare to show a full frontal view of a character. But from the very beginning the Gorgon stared with those hauntingly large eyes directly at the viewer. There is an eeriness, a power, to such depictions, especially the emphasis on the eyes . . . giving one a sense of a creature that could truly turn the beholder to stone."[28]

This feeling probably accounted for much of the popularity of the Gorgoneia. People liked the fact that Medusa's face gave them the creeps in a harmless, ghost-story kind of way. They could shiver under the Gorgon's deadly gaze yet survive to tell the tale—unlike so many less-fortunate victims of the mythological Medusa.

A Changing Face

The scare factor of the Gorgoneia did not last forever. As time passed, artists started to take liberties with the classic Medusa image. Little by little, representations of the Gorgon became less intimidating.

The first wave of change arrived around 500 BC and lasted for several hundred years. During this period Gorgoneia tended to have smaller heads. They were still bodiless, but they did usually have necks. Overall they looked a bit less wild than their predecessors. They still stared straight at the viewer, however, with the typical Medusa glare. Known as middle or transitional Gorgons, these images reflected people's softening attitudes toward the monstrous Medusa.

> ## Did You Know?
> The Gorgoneia and other images used to ward off evil are called apotropaic symbols, from the Greek word *apotropaios*, which means "to turn away."

In years to come these attitudes would shift even further. By about the third century BC, people were starting to think of Medusa as a tragic figure, not just a monster, and the art of the era mirrored this change. Now the creature began to appear in profile or in three-quarter view instead of gazing pop-eyed at the world. Sometimes she was even shown

An Operatic Performance

An opera called *Persée* is among the best known of all Medusa-related stage offerings. Written in 1682 by a French composer named Jean-Baptiste Lully, this work tells the story of Perseus and Andromeda. The Gorgon Medusa plays a prominent role in the story.

Medusa herself appears during the play's third act. The Gorgon sings a song of woe ("J'ai perdue la beauté," which means, "I have lost my beauty") and one of anger ("Je port l'epouvante," which means "I bear terror"). She then falls asleep after the god Mercury sings her a lullaby. Perseus promptly beheads the sleeping monster in a spectacular, bloody scene that includes the birth of Medusa's twin sons from her gory remains. Later Perseus uses Medusa's head to turn a band of marauding soldiers to stone.

Modern audiences can enjoy Lully's opera in all its glory—right on their own television screens! A 2004 performance of *Persée* by the Opera Atelier company of Toronto, Canada, was filmed and released on DVD. Featuring baritone Oliver Laquerre as Medusa, this production sticks closely to the costume and staging traditions of seventeenth-century French opera. Critics praise it as a skillful revival of a centuries-old classic.

asleep, with her eyes closed and her fearful hair at rest. With these changes, the Gorgon was becoming more mortal and less monstrous.

The biggest change of this period, however, went deeper than pose or subject matter. It had to do with Medusa's looks. The Gorgon's fangs, scowl, and protruding tongue disappeared. Her eyes and hair softened, and her face usually wore a sad expression rather than an angry one. As Wilk says, "The Gorgon was no longer a figure of terror, but rather one of pity."[29] It seemed that Medusa was mourning her monstrous nature rather than embracing it.

Images that fit this description are called late or beautiful Gorgons. They were common elements in Greek and Roman art for well over a thousand years. Used to embellish coins, dinnerware, and countless other everyday objects, these pathetic portraits kept the myth of Medusa alive.

Ancient Literature

Art was not the Gorgon's only ticket to extended life. In ancient times Medusa also appeared on the written page. Many long-ago authors employed this monster to more or less faithful degrees in works of literary art.

A famous Greek playwright named Aeschylus was one of the first people to tackle this task. Around the year 500 BC Aeschylus wrote a trilogy of plays that told the story of Perseus. The trilogy's second play, which was titled *The Phorcides*, focused on Perseus's quest for Medusa's head. The full text of this play is now lost, but fragments give historians a glimpse of Aeschylus's ancient tragedy.

Another play by Aeschylus, *Prometheus Bound*, survives today in a more complete form. In this tragedy the main character, Prometheus, warns a maiden named Io that she will probably encounter the dreaded Graeae on her journeys. After escaping the gray witches, Prometheus says, Io must avoid "their three winged sisters, the snake-haired Gorgones, loathed of mankind, whom no one of mortal kind shall look upon and still draw breath. Such is the peril that I bid you to guard against."[30]

A playwright named Euripides also called upon the Medusa mystique. This author's play *Ion*, which was written around 400 BC, concerns in part an assassination attempt. The assassin's weapon is a drop of Medusa's blood, obtained from the goddess Athena. Euripides makes it clear in his dialogue that not only did Athena provide the fatal fluid, but she also struck the blow that set the blood flowing. The Gorgon was "destroyed by Zeus's daughter,"[31] a

Riding the winged white horse Pegasus, a triumphant Perseus displays his trophy: the severed head of Medusa.

character named Creusa announces when asked about the poison she carries.

Passing mentions like these stayed fairly true to the classic Medusa myth. Not all authors, however, were so worried about sticking to the facts. A long-ago novelist named Dionysius Skytobrachion, for example, is known for his wild flights of fancy in regard to many ancient monsters, including Medusa. Skytobrachion's original work is now lost. His ideas have survived, though, because several later historians decided to adopt them as fact. These historians quoted Skytobrachion's work extensively as "proof" that Medusa was more than just a mythical creation.

This was the case with a tale concerning two warlike, all-female African tribes called the Amazons and the Gorgons. Around 50 BC a scholar named Diodorus Siculus recounted Skytobrachion's story in a work called *The Historical Library*. According to Diodorus, the real-life Gorgons were "of great power, till the reign of Medusa, at which time they were conquered by Perseus. At length both they and the Amazons were utterly [exterminated] by Hercules. . . . For it was a thing intolerable to him . . . to suffer any nation to be governed any longer by women."[32]

Modern historians recognize this passage and others like it as pure fiction. In Diodorus's time, however, people were not so sure. They were willing to accept just about any explanation for the terrible Medusa.

Gorgons in the Underworld

Skytobrachion's explanation had roots in reality. Many other authors, however, turned to the supernatural realm for inspiration. During the first century BC a Roman poet named Virgil famously took this approach. In his epic book *Aeneid*, Virgil assigned Gorgons, along with most of Greece's other mythological horrors, to guard the gates of Hell: "Many monstrous forms besides of various beasts are stalled at the doors [of Hades], Centauri and double-shaped Scyllae, and the hundredfold Briareus, and the beast of Lerna, hissing horribly, and the Chimaera armed with flame, Gorgones and Harpyiae, and the shape of the three-bodied shade."[33]

Virgil was not the first author to place Gorgons in the underworld. He was following in the footsteps of Homer, who had made the same assignment centuries earlier. Virgil obviously agreed that Hell was a logical home for Medusa.

Many centuries later a renowned Florentine poet named Dante Alighieri would agree as well. Around AD 1310 Dante wrote the epic poem *The Divine Comedy*, which stands as one of the great classics of Western literature. A segment of this work, titled *Inferno*, describes Dante's imaginary journey through the nine layers of Hell. The poet's tour guide is none other than Virgil, who was apparently considered an expert on all things fiendish.

Virgil shows off this expertise in a segment concerning Medusa. When the episode begins, Dante and Virgil are approaching a city called Dis. There the path is blocked by three ferocious creatures called Furies. The Furies want to kill Dante, but they cannot get close enough. "Let Medusa come and we'll turn him to stone,"[34] they moan in helpless rage.

> ## Did You Know?
> Some scholars believe that early Gorgoneia were inspired by the octopus or squid. They say the snaky hair represents tentacles.

Hearing these words, Virgil takes quick steps to protect Dante. "Turn your back and keep your eyes shut, for if the Gorgon head appears and should you see it, all chance for your return above is lost,"[35] Virgil barks. He grabs Dante by the shoulders and forcibly turns him around. Then he covers Dante's eyes with his own hands to make doubly sure that the poet cannot glimpse the monstrous Gorgon.

These precautions turn out to be unnecessary because Medusa never shows up. Yet it is clear from Dante's words that she lurks somewhere nearby. Just like Homer and Virgil before him, Dante

had consigned the Gorgon to Hell along with other creatures of her awful ilk.

Painting a Monster

Medusa plays a tiny role in *The Divine Comedy*. She only gets a brief mention, and she never makes an actual appearance. Still, Dante's work was a milestone in the Gorgon's history. It brought a fascinating monster back into the public eye after long years of absence—and artists were quick to notice this intriguing new subject. Over the next few centuries many renowned painters turned to Medusa for inspiration.

An Italian artist named Michelangelo Merisi, better known as Caravaggio, was one of these people. In 1597 Caravaggio painted a now-famous image of a shocked-looking Gorgon. The monster's snake-ringed face is lividly, vividly alive—but not, it seems, for long.

Blood streams from Medusa's severed neck, suggesting that the moment of decapitation occurred a mere instant earlier. Angry and appalled, this creature now glares at the world from the walls of the Uffizi Gallery in Florence, Italy.

A few years after Caravaggio unveiled his creation, another striking painting emerged. Titled simply *Medusa*, this work was originally attributed to Leonardo da Vinci. Experts now believe, however, that it was painted by an anonymous Flemish artist. The piece shows Medusa's severed head lying on a floor, grimacing as if in pain. A tangled mass of hissing, biting snakes erupts from the head. As one critic says colorfully, they are "strangling each other in terrified struggle to come from the Medusa brain."[36] Bats, lizards, frogs, rats, and other creatures of the night hover nearby, calmly watching the gruesome scene. They seem to feel right at home in the presence of the Gorgon's horrible death.

The same is true of another Flemish painting titled *Tête de Méduse* (French for *Medusa's Head*). Created in 1618 by Peter Paul Rubens, this work is suspiciously similar to the anonymous painting just described. It too features a severed head with a horrified expression, frantic serpents, and various animal attendants. The scene is shown from a different angle, however, emphasizing Medusa's face rather than her snaky locks. Frozen in terror, this face captures the brutal moment of the Gorgon's death.

> **Did You Know?**
> In the 1600s and 1700s, the myth of Perseus, Andromeda, and Medusa inspired more than 25 operas.

Sadness rather than terror is the theme of yet another famous Medusa portrait. Swiss artist Arnold Böcklin's *Medusa*, painted in 1878, is a full-face image that brings the ancient Gorgoneia to mind. In this work Medusa's snaky locks are relaxed, falling in carefully arranged ringlets around the Gorgon's head. Deep-set eyes stare mournfully out of a face so sad, so tragic that viewers are forced to feel sorry for the Gorgon and her wretched life.

This classic image is arresting not only for its sadness but also for its perfection. The features and skin are so flawless that they seem to be sculpted from stone. Forever frozen on canvas, the Gorgon shares the fate of her many human victims.

Medusa in Sculpture

As striking as it is, Böcklin's Medusa only *looks* like stone. Many other artists took the concept a step further: They used actual stone or other solid media to create their Gorgons. Sculpted to endure through the ages, these creations are lasting tributes to one of mythology's greatest monsters.

Many Medusa sculptures depict the moment of the Gorgon's beheading. Of all these works, Benvenuto Cellini's *Perseus* (also sometimes called *Persus Beheading Medusa*) is undoubtedly the most famous. Created in 1554, this massive bronze work stands in the Piazza della Signoria in Florence, Italy. It shows Perseus holding a sword in one hand and raising Medusa's severed head with the other. The hero stands atop the Gorgon's writhing body, pinning it to the ground with one strong foot.

Cellini's statue fascinates art historians for many reasons. One of them is the artist's depiction of Medusa, who in this piece is beautiful to the point of perfection. A critic describes the Gorgon with these words:

> The body of Medusa is sculpted with loving care. She is not a monster, as legend would have her, but a woman; headless of course, but a beautiful woman. . . . Medusa's head . . . is not a monster's head. . . . Its sensual beauty is truly stunning: eyes closed, mouth half open, a hint of teeth, the oval of the face framed in a mesh of snakes above and the folds of the skin at the neck wound.[37]

Another famous statue created centuries later takes a similar approach to Medusa's appearance. Antonio Canova's *Perseus with the Head of Medusa*, which was carved from marble between 1804 and 1806, also shows a sword-bearing Perseus raising a classically lovely Gorgon head. Yet instead of looking calm, as in Cellini's work, Me-

The Medusa Shield

A book of biographies from the mid-1500s tells the story of a Medusa-like monster painted on a belt buckle by a young Leonardo da Vinci. The author describes Leonardo's work with these words:

> He began to think what he could paint . . . that might be able to terrify all who should come upon it, producing the same effect as once did the head of Medusa. For this purpose, then, Leonardo [gathered] lizards great and small, crickets, serpents, butterflies, grasshoppers, bats, and other strange kinds of suchlike animals . . . out of the number of which, variously put together, he formed a great ugly creature, most horrible and terrifying, which emitted a poisonous breath and turned the air to flame; and he made it coming out of a dark and jagged rock, belching forth venom from its open throat, fire from its eyes, and smoke from its nostrils.
>
> When Leonardo finished his painting, he called his father into the studio. The elder man took a step backwards, startled, when he spotted the horrible apparition—and Leonardo just smiled. "This work serves the end for which it was made; take it, then, and carry it away, since this is the effect that it was meant to produce," he said with satisfaction.
>
> Leonardo da Vinci's Medusa shield, as it is known today, is lost. Historians question whether it ever really existed. Yet the story survives as one of the art world's most intriguing mysteries.

Giorgio Vasari, *Lives of the Most Excellent Painters, Sculptors, and Architects*, 1568, in *Stories of the Italian Artists from Vasari*, trans. E.L. Seeley. New York: Duffield, 1913, p. 147.

dusa's expression is sad and very human. The Gorgon seems to be mourning the moment of her death.

Even at this point, however, the monster may be striking a final blow. Canova's Perseus is, after all, locked in stone for all eternity—and at least one art critic feels that the artist was well aware of this irony. In Canova's interpretation, points out this critic, "Perseus dares to look at the head of Medusa (most incarnations of the hero do not) as if there were nothing more to fear from her gaze."[38] The sly suggestion is that there was, after all, something to fear. Perseus's marble figure stands as proof that one cannot look upon Medusa, even in death, and live to tell the tale.

Medusa in Architecture

Cellini, Canova, and countless others created art for art's sake. Not all artists, however, took such a lofty approach. Paintings, carvings, and other creations had many practical uses. They decorated walls and gates, they formed columns and roofs, and they even channeled water. Medusa's image has been meeting these and other architectural needs since the myth of the Gorgon first appeared.

One famous piece of Medusa-related architecture appears on the remains of the ancient Temple of Artemis. The temple's pediment, which is the triangular piece under the roof, bears the carved image of an archaic-style Gorgon. The monster is clearly meant to be Medusa because it holds the infant Chrysaor in one outstretched hand. The creature's other arm also curves outward and probably held Pegasus at one time. Now on display at the Archaeological Museum of Corfu, Greece, the Corfu pediment is one of the best surviving examples of Medusa in ancient architecture.

> # Did You Know?
>
> Medusa was a popular theme for poets of the Romantic era, which spanned the years of the late 1700s and the early to middle 1800s.

The Greek hero Perseus raises Medusa's severed head for all to see in this massive bronze sculpture done by Benvenuto Cellini in 1554. The sculpture still stands in Florence, Italy.

Many old mosaic floors also survive. Most mosaic Gorgons are heads surrounded by circular designs, evoking the image of Athena's shield. One well-known mosaic, on display today at the Athens Archaeological Museum in Greece, shows a sad-eyed Medusa with wings growing from her forehead and long, snaky locks writhing around her temples. Other mosaics show thoughtful Medusas, beautiful Medusas, angry Medusas, and everything in between. As one type of Gorgoneia, these patterns were meant to protect the people who trod upon them.

The Gorgons that decorated walls and gates had a similar purpose. Again taking the familiar shape of Gorgoneia, these symbols glared threateningly at the outside world. They were thought to drive away evil and keep the residents safe. The stunning golden Medusa shield that decorates the main gate of the royal palace in Turin, Italy, is one striking example of this usage.

Not quite as splendid, but equally remarkable, are the Gorgon-themed gargoyles that appear on churches and other buildings throughout the Western world. With their gaping mouths, these stone statues have a practical purpose: They channel rainwater off roofs. As author Stephen King points out, however, they have a symbolic purpose as well: "Their horrible, stony faces offer a unique catharsis; when we look upon them and shudder, we create the exact reversal of the Medusa myth; we are not flesh turned to stone, but flesh proving it is flesh still."[39] By placing this monster on houses of worship, ancient architects thus reminded people of their mortality—and also cautioned them about the horrors that awaited wrongdoers in the afterlife.

Modern Art

In modern times artists in many different media have continued to send this message. Medusa was portrayed by some of the twentieth century's most renowned painters, including Pablo Picasso, Paul Klee, John Singer Sargent, and others. She has been re-created in bronze by the Spanish artist Salvador Dalí. She also appears in sculptor Auguste Rodin's towering tribute to Dante's *Divine Comedy*. Titled *The Gates of Hell*, this masterwork was originally sculpted from plaster, then cast in bronze. Replicas stand today in several cities around the world, giving delicious chills to thousands of viewers each year.

The Gorgon's image is not just found in museums. As in ages past, it shows up in everyday venues as well. Architects still build Gorgoneia into walls, gates, and floors, especially in Greece. Countless Web sites and sidewalk art shows feature the Medusa-inspired creations of everyday artists. The Gorgon's face even appears on the flag of Sicily, Italy. Officially adopted in 2000, this flag presumably serves a function very similar to that of the ancient Gorgoneia. Flying above every Sicilian government building, Medusa's image keeps the region's citizens safe from harm.

It is hardly surprising that the Gorgon is still turning up in these ways. Medusa's story may be well known, but the monster is nonetheless a blank slate in many ways. Her face and her story can mean different things to different people. The Gorgon therefore provides an unending source of creative ideas. Scary but stimulating, this mythical monster surely will continue to inspire future generations of artists.

Chapter 4

Medusa in Popular Culture

I n some ways Medusa is like an elderly movie star. She has had a long career during which her popularity has waxed and waned. During some eras, such as the heydays of ancient Greece and Rome, *everyone* knew the monster's name and face. In other periods, such as the early Christian centuries, Medusa was mostly forgotten. She lurked in dusty books on library shelves during these times, just waiting for a chance to burst back into prominence.

The Gorgon has gotten this chance in modern times. She is now better known than perhaps ever before. From novels and movies to comics and even video games, Medusa slithers her way into every nook and cranny of modern popular culture.

A Novel Approach

A couple of early fictional adaptations laid the groundwork for this comeback. One of these works was a 1933 short story called "Shambleau," written by Catherine L. Moore. This story concerns a space cowboy named Northwest Smith who saves a creepy female alien while wandering on Mars. The monster has glorious red hair that turns into snake-like, entangling locks when she wants to feed on a human victim—who, in this case, is the unlucky Smith. The feeding is deadly, but pleasurable, and Northwest Smith falls deeper and deeper under the Gorgon's spell. He is finally rescued by his friend Yarl, who shoots the creature with a ray gun while watching her reflection in a mirror.

One literary blogger points out that this story was not simply a good read. It also broke new ground where the Medusa mystique was concerned. "The . . . Medusa thing is old stuff. It goes way back. By transposing it to Mars, Moore manages to revitalize . . . the old myths and accomplishes the seemingly impossible task of making it work here-and-now. . . . [It is] creepy and horrifically effective all over again,"[40] he explains.

A 1935 novel titled *The Circus of Dr. Lao* accomplished a similar goal. Written by Charles Grandison Finney, this book's plot centers around a Chinese showman named Dr. Lao. Lao has created a circus chock-full of mythological creatures instead of elephants, lions, and other more typical beasts. One of Lao's creatures is Medusa, who is described as "a Sonoran medusa from Northern Mexico."[41] Medusa has several species of Mexican snakes for hair and, like the mythological Gorgon, has the power to turn viewers to stone.

> # Did You Know?
> In modern times Medusa's severed head has become a popular feminist icon, representing female rage.

This power creates a quandary for Dr. Lao because his captive Medusa is part of a public display and is meant to be seen. The doctor addresses the problem by placing a large mirror next to Medusa's pen. He ropes off the pen so that the audience can see Medusa's reflection but not her actual body. In this way they can marvel without fear at the Gorgon and her monstrous looks.

This setup usually keeps everyone safe. Occasionally, though, someone decides to ignore Dr. Lao's guidelines. In one gruesome scene, a viewer slips past the ropes to get a closer look at Medusa. The results are not surprising. The foolish woman stiffens into stone as soon as she lays eyes on the Gorgon. This fictional victim stands as proof that even in modern times, Medusa still holds the power of life or death in her horrible hands.

Medusa on Film

The same is true in *7 Faces of Dr. Lao*, a 1964 film loosely based on Finney's book. Directed by George Pal and starring Tony Randall and Barbara Eden, this movie features a cheesy Medusa capped with rubber snakes. Despite the Gorgon's cobbled-together costume, critics were generally forgiving. "It helps that the character is seen only in a mirror or in quick cuts, and that the rubber snakes vibrate in a motion that, under such circumstances, looks believable,"[42] admits one writer.

Anything but believable was *Medusa Against the Son of Hercules*, another film released around the same time. This movie was made for television along with 14 other "Sons of Hercules" films during the mid-1960s. The Medusa entry in this franchise is a campy classic featuring secondhand costumes and sets, bad dialogue, and questionable acting. It attempts to tell the story of Perseus and Andromeda, touching on the Gorgon and other mythological monsters in the process.

Although this film stays true to the Perseus myth in many ways, Medusa's looks are a significant departure. The movie features an inexplicable Gorgon that, says one critic, "is NOT a woman with snakes all over her head. . . . The Medusa here is a tree-like creature with a large glowing orange eye that lives in a dry lake bed."[43] The tree-Gorgon is able to turn people to stone, though, and she uses her petrifying power several times throughout the movie. Awful yet amusing, this picture holds a beloved place in the hearts of movie Medusa fans everywhere.

Another movie, *The Gorgon*, was filmed in 1964 and produced by Hammer Studios. In this movie a modern-day Medusa leaves her lair to terrorize a nearby town whenever the full moon shines. These

> ## Did You Know?
>
> In the 1935 book *The Circus of Dr. Lao*, by Charles Grandison Finney, Medusa has three types of snakes in her hair: black-headed snakes, night snakes, and glossy snakes.

Named After a Monster

Medusa has snaked her way into every aspect of modern-day life, even the scientific realm. She is especially prominent under the sea, where various creatures go by the Gorgon's name.

Certain adult jellyfish are in this group. Fully mature jellies with umbrella-shaped bodies and dangling tentacles are known as Medusae. In most species, the tentacles can deliver a painful sting. Much like the original Medusa's biting snakes, these deadly tendrils keep foolish humans from getting too close.

Gorgonians also bring the Gorgon to mind. These multibranched soft corals dot the reefs of the world. Their thick, semirigid arms look a bit like the snakes that erupt from Medusa's head, and the coral probably gets its name from this resemblance.

Some dictionaries point out that the word *gorgon* meant "coral" in Latin. This fact provides a simple explanation for the gorgonian's name. The deeper connection, though, is interesting to explore. Ancient tales claim that Medusa's head, her blood, or both actually created the world's coral. It is likely that this incident crept into the Latin language. The Latin *gorgon*, therefore, has a direct link to Greece's most famous monster.

excursions leave a string of stony victims that baffle everyone—until, that is, a noted scientist arrives on the scene. Much speculation, sleuthing, and stealth lead to a final and dramatic confrontation with the gruesome Gorgon.

This film got mixed reviews. Critics agreed that it was interesting and beautifully filmed. Yet they generally felt that it was memorably weak in the special-effects department. Actor Christopher

Lee, who played Medusa's scientist nemesis in the movie, agreed wholeheartedly. "Beautiful-looking picture, but the whole thing fell apart because the effect of the snakes on [Medusa's] head was not sufficiently well done,"[44] he remembered in a 1983 interview.

Clash of the Titans

The special effects continued to be a topic of conversation in the next Medusa-related offering to hit the big screen. The 1981 *Clash of the Titans* was yet another retelling of the Perseus and Andromeda myth. It featured actors and animated beasts. The movie's monsters were created using a technique called stop-action animation, which uses clay models repositioned and photographed over and over to mimic motion.

Opinions are divided about this technique. Some viewers find the effect jerky and clumsy. Others think it is unique and fun. "I don't care what anyone says, no multi-million-dollar special effect can ever be as cool as the stop-motion effects used in this movie. Some might say that it's dated. Well perhaps it is, but they did such a great job in creating the monsters (especially Medusa) that one can only marvel at them,"[45] writes one happy viewer.

The general public obviously agreed because the movie was a modest commercial success. Viewers enjoyed the film's plot, which stuck fairly close to the classic Greek version of the tale. They also liked the movie's Medusa, who was satisfyingly beastly. This Gorgon had scaly, reptilian skin and a strikingly ugly face. Her head was ringed with thick, writhing serpents that hissed and bit at the air, and her eyes glowed bright green when she used her petrifying powers.

Did You Know?

Carlo Rambaldi, the artist who created the tree-Gorgon in the 1963 film *Medusa Against the Son of Hercules,* went on to design special effects for blockbusters such as *E.T.: The Extraterrestrial* and *Alien.*

This effect figured prominently in one of the film's biggest moments. Having obtained the Gorgon's head, Perseus rushes to rescue Andromeda from the sea monster known as the Kraken. Arriving in the nick of time, Perseus raises Medusa's severed head. The creature's dead eyes start to shoot brilliant beams of light—and caught in the glare, the Kraken freezes. Bit by bit, the huge sea monster hardens into rock. His giant body then crumbles into the sea, where it can never bother Andromeda or Perseus again.

This scene and others got a face lift in 2010, when *Clash of the Titans* was remade using modern special-effects techniques. The revamped offering features possibly the scariest Medusa ever to appear on film. From the waist up, this Gorgon is a stunningly

Human actors and animated beasts brought to life a retelling of the Perseus and Andromeda myth in the 1981 film Clash of the Titans. *The film's Medusa (pictured) had scaly, reptilian skin and the characteristic writhing serpents ringing her head.*

beautiful woman with serpentine locks. Below the waist, she is a massive snake. She slithers with lightning speed through her underground lair, chasing Perseus and a team of human hunters. One by one she corners Perseus's friends—and at these moments, Medusa's true nature reveals itself. The creature changes from a gorgeous girl into a hideous hag, and her deadly eyes light up. Stony transformations immediately ensue.

The Lightning Thief

Both *Clash of the Titans* films told the Medusa story much as it appears in Greek mythology. Another 2010 movie, however, took a much more fanciful approach. In *Percy Jackson and the Olympians: The Lightning Thief*, Perseus is renamed "Percy" and morphs into a modern high-school-age boy. Percy is a demigod—the offspring of a human and a god. He and his half-blood friends have many heroic adventures, one of which is a scary encounter with the Gorgon Medusa.

This encounter does not take place in the typical dark cave. It occurs in rural New Jersey, where Medusa owns a store called "Aunty Em's Gnome Emporium." The store sells astonishingly lifelike stone statues. Medusa secretly creates these statues in her backyard garden, where she traps and then petrifies clueless human victims.

The face-off between Percy and Medusa occurs in this garden. Percy hides desperately behind one statue after another, trying to avoid the Gorgon's gaze. To keep track of the monster, he activates his cell phone's mirror application. He angles the phone so he can see Medusa's reflection, just as the mythological Perseus did with Athena's polished shield. Percy eventually manages to behead his pursuer, forever putting "Aunty Em" out of the garden gnome business.

Did You Know?

Award-winning designer Ray Harryhausen created the stop-motion effects for the 1981 version of *Clash of the Titans*. This film was Harryhausen's last major project.

In this film Medusa is played by award-winning actress Uma Thurman. Thurman hints at the Gorgon's monstrous nature through many quirky mannerisms, including a subtle but oddly menacing head jerk. In a 2010 video interview, Thurman explained how she developed this trait. "I had a snake wrangler bring in a whole number of live snakes which we handled and played with just because I wanted to get a realistic [view], to imagine how heavy it would be, like what do these things weigh? They weigh a lot,"[46] she laughed, bobbing her head to illustrate her words.

The result of Thurman's research is surprisingly effective. Her Medusa does seem to be carrying a heavy load that she cannot entirely control. The serpents wriggle, and the Gorgon's head lurches in response. It is easy to see how this annoying hairdo could put its owner into a permanently monstrous mood.

Modern Reads for All Ages

Like many of today's movies, *The Lightning Thief* did not originate in Hollywood. It started as a young-adult novel. Published in 2005, the book of the same name by author Rick Riordan was the first entry in a whole series of Percy Jackson tales.

The Medusa who appears in Riordan's books is arguably the best-known Gorgon of the modern literary world. She is not, however, the only one. Several other noted authors have brought this monster to fictional life.

An American writer named John Barth is one of these authors. In 1972 Barth wrote *Chimera*, a National Book Award–winning novel that contains three loosely linked stories. The novel's second story, "Perseid," is written from the point of view of a now middle-aged Perseus who feels old, fat, and unheroic. When he finds out that Athena brought Medusa back to life and gave her the power to make people young instead of statuesque, Perseus embarks on a new quest for the Gorgon. He and Medusa end up falling in love and turning into starry constellations. They live happily ever after in the sky, where they proudly display their union for all the world to see.

The Gorgon's search for love is also a theme in *The Source of Magic*, a novel in the Xanth series by popular science-fiction author Piers Anthony. First published in 1979, this book concerns a naive and lonely Medusa who does not recognize her own powers. When a visitor asks the Gorgon where all her suitors have gone, she just sighs. "They went away. The men left the gifts behind, pictures of themselves, sculptures,"[47] she explains sadly, gesturing to the rocky forms that surround her abode. Medusa does not realize that these sculptures *are* her suitors. She cannot understand why she has so much trouble finding—and keeping—a good man.

In more recent years, author Ross Collins's *Medusa Jones* has introduced a new generation of readers to the Gorgon. This 2008 book's elementary-age heroine, Medusa, is the granddaughter of the original Medusa. Her home is amusingly surrounded by the stony forms of postmen, gardeners, and other visitors who have come a little too close during "Gran's" visits. Young Medusa can petrify things too, but her parents disapprove of such shenanigans. They

Unsuspecting visitors turn to stone after gazing at Medusa in a scene from the 2010 movie Percy Jackson and the Olympians: The Lightning Thief. *In the movie, Medusa, played by Uma Thurman, sells these amazingly lifelike statues at her New Jersey store.*

stubbornly forbid their daughter to turn anything, especially her annoying classmates, into stone.

Comics and Cartoons

No such constraints exist in the world of comics and cartoons. Consumers of these media formats clamor to see every gory detail of monstrous confrontations. They want to watch Medusa performing every evil act she can possibly muster.

This need is met most prominently in the Marvel Universe, a fictional world created by graphic-arts powerhouse Marvel Comics. In this collection, Medusa is a member of the Inhumans' royal family. Her primary power, explains Marvel's Web site, is the ability to "control the rate of growth and movement of each strand of her tougher-than-steel hair individually. She maintains this control even when the hair has been cut from her head."[48] Medusa uses her snake-like hair to catch and subdue her foes, thus causing endless trouble for the Fantastic Four and other well-meaning heroes.

> ## Did You Know?
>
> In the 2010 movie *Percy Jackson and the Olympians: The Lightning Thief,* Uma Thurman's Medusa wears a black head scarf and dark sunglasses to disguise her true nature during business hours.

More classic elements appear in a graphic novel titled *Wonder Woman: Eyes of the Gorgon.* Published in 2005, this 192-page tome features an original story line by noted comic author Greg Rucka. The book's highlight is a fight to the death between Wonder Woman and Medusa. Wonder Woman triumphs in the end, but she loses her sight in the process. She must blind herself to avoid the Gorgon's deadly gaze.

Snake Face, a character that appeared in the 2002 season of the animated television series *He-Man and the Masters of the Universe,* also boasts classic Gorgon powers. This inhuman creature is covered with snakes from the shoulders up. These snakes can petrify anyone their owner hates or fears, and Snake Face uses this ability to good effect throughout the season. He is finally conquered, however, when He-Man tricks him into viewing his own reflection in a mirrored shield. Faced with his own terrible gaze, Snake Face promptly turns to stone.

Horrifying Games

The popularity of stories like these proves that Medusa still has the power to fascinate—and it is not hard to see why. The Gorgon may be frightening, but she is also, as one author says, "just a real cool monster."[49] Medusa has powers that many people would love to claim for themselves.

The role-playing game *Dungeons & Dragons* gives players the chance to dabble in these powers. First introduced in 1974, this game now boasts an estimated 20 million players worldwide. Some editions of the game let players assume the role of Medusa, whose abilities vary depending on the package. In editions 3 and 3.5, for instance, Medusa has a petrifying gaze, and her snaky hair delivers venomous bites. In later editions Medusa can use blood drops to bring her victims back to life. This character and her supernatural powers have been enthusiastically received by *Dungeons & Dragons* enthusiasts.

Audiences have also embraced video games, which provide their own unique spin on the Medusa myth. The *Castlevania* series, for example, has been using Medusa as a recurring enemy since the franchise first appeared in 1986. The Gorgon appears as a snake-like person or, sometimes, as a gigantic staring head.

A 2005 game called *God of War* also places Medusa in a prominent role. The main character in this game, Kratos, can use the Gor-

> ## Did You Know?
>
> Medusa appears in a 1937 Warner Brothers cartoon titled "Porky's Hero Agency." Porky Pig dreams that he is a Greek hero who must defeat a not-so-scary Gorgon.

Ride the Beast

Many scary amusement park rides have been inspired by fictional and mythical monsters. Medusa is one of these monsters. The Gorgon lends her name and face to a floorless roller coaster at Six Flags Discovery Kingdom in Vallejo, California. Featuring a 150-foot (46m) drop, 7 inversions, and a top speed of 65 miles per hour (105kph), this ride offers scares of a type the original Gorgon could never match. "Look fear right in the eye," the coaster's promotional materials taunt in a subtle reference to Medusa's petrifying powers.

Another coaster named Medusa can be found at Six Flags Mexico in Mexico City. Introduced in 2000, this ride is a wooden coaster that boasts more than half a mile (800m) of coiling, serpentine trails. Typical of wooden coasters, the ride is rough and jerky—and it is also fast. With a top speed of 55 miles per hour (89kph), this Gorgon takes riders on a journey their stomachs will never forget.

gon's petrifying power as a weapon, but he must kill the monster to get it. "I offer you the power to freeze your enemies where they stand, but you must earn such a gift," whispers the goddess Aphrodite in the early stages of the game. "Medusa, the Queen of the Gorgons. Bring me her head, Kratos, and I will give you the ability to wield its power."[50] Players must obey Aphrodite's command and slay the Gorgon or die in the attempt.

Other Uses

Most modern Medusa seekers, luckily, do not risk such dire consequences. To find the Gorgon, all they need to do is turn on the television or drive to a local store, because today Medusa's image is everywhere. This Greek horror shows up in Halloween displays and on the Sunday comics page. Her snaky hair inspires characters and moments in countless television shows, movies, and cartoons. Medusa lends her name to a popular makeup company, and she is even the face of the Versace fashion and accessories line. In a 1996 interview, Gianni Versace explained the reasons behind this choice: "Medusa means attraction . . . a *dangerous* attraction."[51]

This comment points out a key aspect of Medusa's appeal: The monster is snake-like in her power to charm. Even though people throughout history have understood the Gorgon's deadly nature, they cannot seem to avert their eyes. They *will* brave Medusa's gaze. If they are lucky, these people will emerge unharmed. If not, they will fall under the Gorgon's spell—figuratively, at least. As long as mortals dare to look Medusa in the eye, this monster is sure to maintain her rock-hard hold on peoples' imaginations—and to live on in their worst nightmares.

Source Notes

Chapter One: Making a Monster

1. Homer, *The Iliad*, bk. 5, Literature Network. www.online-literature.com.
2. Homer, *The Iliad*, bk. 6.
3. Homer, *The Odyssey*, bk. 11, Literature Network. www.online-literature. com.
4. Hesiod, *Shield of Heracles*, in *The Homeric Hymns and Homerica*, trans. Hugh G. Evelyn-White. Cambridge, MA: Harvard University Press, 1982, Theoi Greek Mythology. www.theoi.com.
5. Stephen R. Wilk, *Medusa: Solving the Mystery of the Gorgon*. New York: Oxford University Press, 2000, p. 18.
6. Ovid, *Metamorphoses*, trans. Brookes More, bk. 4. Boston: Cornhill, 1922, lines 793–96, Theoi Greek Mythology. www.theoi.com.
7. Ovid, *Metamorphoses*, trans. More, lines 799–800.
8. Achilles Tatius, *The Adventures of Leucippe and Clitophon*, trans. John Winkler, in Marjorie Garber and Nancy J. Vickers, eds., *The Medusa Reader*. New York: Routledge, 2003, pp. 45–46.
9. Apollodorus, *The Library*, trans. James George Frazer, vols. 121 and 122. Cambridge, MA: Harvard University Press, 1921, Theoi Greek Mythology. www.theoi.com.
10. Hesiod, *Theogony*, in *The Homeric Hymns and Homerica*.
11. Lucan, *Pharsalia*, trans. Robert Graves, in Marjorie Garber and Nancy J. Vickers, eds., *The Medusa Reader*. New York: Routledge, 2003, p. 41.
12. Ovid, *Metamorphoses*, trans. More, lines 651–62.
13. Ovid, *Metamorphoses*, trans. Rolfe Humphries, in Marjorie Garber and Nancy J. Vickers, eds., *The Medusa Reader*. New York: Routledge, 2003, p. 31.
14. Marjorie Garber and Nancy J. Vickers, eds., *The Medusa Reader*. New York: Routledge, 2003, p. 2.

Chapter Two: Perseus and Medusa

15. Apollodorus, *The Library*.
16. Apollodorus, *The Library*.
17. Wilk, *Medusa*, p. 20.
18. Apollodorus, *The Library*.
19. Apollodorus, *The Library*.
20. Ovid, *Metamorphoses*, trans. Humphries, p. 35.
21. Apollodorus, *The Library*.
22. Hesiod, *Shield of Heracles*.
23. Ovid, *Metamorphoses*, trans. Humphries, p. 37.
24. Ovid, *Metamorphoses*, trans. Humphries, p. 38.
25. Ovid, *Metamorphoses*, trans. Humphries, p. 39.
26. Ovid, *Metamorphoses*, trans. Humphries, p. 39.
27. Apollodorus, *The Library*.

Chapter Three: Medusa in Art, Literature, and Theater

28. Wilk, *Medusa*, p. 31.
29. Wilk, *Medusa*, p. 35.
30. Aeschylus, *Prometheus Bound*, trans. H.W. Smith, vols. 145 and 146. Cambridge, MA: Harvard University Press, 1926, fragment 790, Theoi Greek Mythology. www.theoi.com.
31. Euripides, *Ion*, trans. Ronald Frederick Willetts, in Marjorie Garber and Nancy J. Vickers, eds., *The Medusa Reader*. New York: Routledge, 2003, p. 17.
32. Diodorus Siculus, *The Historical Library*, trans. G. Booth, in Marjorie Garber and Nancy J. Vickers, eds., *The Medusa Reader*. New York: Routledge, 2003, p. 29.
33. Virgil, *Eclogues, Georgics, Aeneid*, trans. H.R. Fairclough, vols. 63 and 64, bk. 6. Cambridge, MA: Harvard University Press, 1916, fragment 287, Theoi Greek Mythology. www.theoi.com.
34. Dante, *The Divine Comedy*, trans. Robert Hollander and Jean Hollander, Princeton Dante Project, canto 9, line 52. http://etc web.princeton.edu.
35. Dante, *The Divine Comedy*, canto 9, lines 55–57.
36. Walter Pater, *The Renaissance*. London: Macmillan, 1900, p. 106.

37. Ugo Bardi, "Cellini's Medusa." Chimaera, August 2003. www.unifi.it.

38. Hal Foster, *Prosthetic Gods*. Cambridge, MA: MIT Press, 2004, pp. 257–58.

39. Stephen King, *Nightmares in the Sky: Gargoyles and Grotesques*. New York: Viking Studio Books, 1988, p. 35.

Chapter Four: Medusa in Popular Culture

40. NetherWerks, "Shambleau," *Old School Heretic,* November 11, 2010. http://oldschoolheretic.blogspot.com.

41. Quoted in Wilk, *Medusa,* p. 201.

42. Wilk, *Medusa,* p. 203.

43. Chris Jarmick, "Review of *Medusa Against the Son of Hercules,*" Epinions, October 31, 2006. www.epinions.com.

44. Quoted in Internet Movie Database, "*The Gorgon*: Trivia." www.imdb.com.

45. Eric F., "Simply an Excellent Viewing Experience," Amazon.com reviews, March 18, 2004. www.amazon.com.

46. Uma Thurman, interview, "On Her Preparation Work with Actual Snakes," Internet Movie Database, 2010. www.imdb.com.

47. Piers Anthony, *The Source of Magic*. New York: Del Ray, 1979, p. 141.

48. Marvel Universe Wiki, "Medusa: Powers," Marvel. http://marvel.com.

49. Wilk, *Medusa,* p. 224.

50. Quoted in God of War Wiki, "Medusa's Gaze," Wikia. http://godofwar.wikia.com.

51. Quoted in Mark Seal, "The Versace Moment," 1996, in Marjorie Garber and Nancy J. Vickers, eds., *The Medusa Reader*. New York: Routledge, 2003, p. 276.

For Further Exploration

Books

Stephen Batchelor, *The Ancient Greeks for Dummies*. Chichester, England: John Wiley & Sons, 2008. This entertaining guide introduces readers to the world of ancient Greece, including the era's mythological beliefs.

Zachary Hamby, *Mythology for Teens: Classic Myths in Today's World*. Austin, TX: Prufrock, 2009. This book helps readers to relate the themes of ancient Greek stories, including the tale of Perseus and Medusa, to modern issues.

Edith Hamilton, *Mythology: Timeless Tales of Gods and Heroes*. New York: Penguin, 1942. This book is a classic. It contains key retellings of many Greek tales, including the myth of Perseus and Medusa.

Sophia Kelly, *What a Beast! A Look-It-Up Guide to the Monsters and Mutants of Mythology*. New York: Franklin Watts, 2009. Loaded with facts about ancient Greece's scariest monsters, including Medusa, this book is a fun read for kids and grown-ups alike.

Stephen King, *Nightmares in the Sky: Gargoyles and Grotesques*. New York: Viking Studio Books, 1988. This book is a classic photographic study of Gorgon and other gargoyles around the world.

Websites

Greek Mythology (www.greekmythology.com). This website includes extensive information on the monsters, heroes, gods, and stories of ancient Greece.

Monster Librarian (www.monsterlibrarian.com). This site offers reviews and information on horror books of all types, along with many good articles and author interviews.

Poetry Foundation (www.poetryfoundation.org). This site includes a vast collection of modern poetry. Search for "Medusa" to find more than 100 poems that refer to this creature.

Project Gutenberg (www.gutenberg.org). This website offers free full-text versions of more than 100,000 classic works, including many ancient Greek writings.

Theoi Greek Mythology (www.theoi.com). This site is a wonderful resource for information about the characters and episodes in Greek mythology. It includes an extensive collection of ancient writings on Perseus and Medusa.

Index

Picture Credits

Cover: Galleria degli Uffizi, Florence, Italy/The Bridgeman Art Library International

© Bettmann/Corbis: 43

Bibliotheque des Arts Decoratifs, Paris, France/Archives Charmet/The Bridgeman Art Library International: 35

Bpk, Berlin/Art Resource, NY: 28

Henry Matthew Brock/The Bridgeman Art Library International: 17

© Elio Ciol/Corbis: 11

Johnny van Haeften Gallery, London, UK/The Bridgeman Art Library International: 46

Erich Lessing/Art Resource, NY: 7

Gilles Mermet/Art Resource, NY: 39

Photofeat: 59, 62

Thinkstock/AbleStock.com: 51

About the Author

Kris Hirschmann has written more than 200 books for children. She owns and runs a business that provides a variety of writing and editorial services. She lives just outside Orlando, Florida, with her husband, Michael, and her daughters Nikki and Erika.